Learn to Read with Great Speed

How to Take Your Reading Skills to the Next Level and Beyond in only 10 Minutes a Day

By Michal Stawicki

www.expandbeyondyourself.com

2

Table of Contents

4

About the Author 53

Introduction

This is my second book in the "10 minute" series. There is some redundancy between this one and The Fitness Expert Next Door in the second chapter, so if you read that one - you were warned.

When I started my self-development program, I stumbled upon a workbook about speed reading. The author outlined a program there for a massive improvement in the speed of reading within three months, but you were supposed to practice one to two hours per day, every day.

Two hours per day! That's a lot of commitment. I didn't have time for it. But I was at a stage of developing my Ten-Minute Philosophy and decided to give it a try, but only for 10 minutes a day. I took that program and modified it by extending each week into a full twelve weeks.

The last time I checked my reading speed, I read at about 240 words per minute. Since that time, my skills had no chance to improve, as I was reading less rather than more and neglected any training in that area.

I checked my results after a month from starting my 10-minute practices, and I was blown away! It was 360 words per minute, 50% progress! Later on, it appeared this result was a coincidence, but still, after six weeks of practice, I read about 340 words per minute, and the progress was impressive.

All you need to achieve similar results is this booklet and 10 minutes a day of your time.

I want to help you, not to rob you. If you can already read quickly, or if you read no more than 30 minutes a day, then the program described below won't improve your skills or give you profits. Remember that I speak of all the time you commit to reading as a whole. That includes Internet, magazines, mail, and work materials, not just reading for pleasure in your leisure time.

So, reader, how fast do you read? If you don't know, then check it out immediately:
http://www.staples.com/sbd/cre/marketing/technology-research-centers/ereaders/speed-reader/
OR
http://legge.psych.umn.edu/mnread/DEMO_RS/

If you are offline and cannot reach those online tests, then prepare a timer, and read below four paragraphs highlighted in different font. Start a timer, and read the paragraphs at a fast enough pace to comprehend the meaning. Then, use the formula I provided after those paragraphs to gauge your reading speed. Ready? Go:

If your honest result is below two hundred and fifty words per minute, then this book is the

best value available for you. Grab it, practice ten minutes a day, and within several weeks, you will experience a significant improvement of your reading skills.

If you read below four hundreds words per minute, then I still encourage you to give my ten-minute program a try. You don't have much to lose, and you have a lot to gain: your precious time. You could read the same amount of text in 2/3 of time previously needed. Or you can read twenty, forty, or one hundred percent more text at the same time.

If you read faster than four hundred words per minute, then I cannot guarantee that the techniques I recommend will significantly improve your reading speed. But if you've never consciously worked on your reading skills, then chances are that you have a natural talent and you can develop it with a few simple, consistent exercises. Try it for thirty days. All you've got to lose is one dollar and five hours of your time within a month. The average American spends more time in front of the TV in two days[1] And the potential gains are huge.

Generally, the slower you read right now, the bigger gains of increasing your skill are. Using my example - I read two hundred and forty words per minute, and I would read about two

---

[1] http://www.bls.gov/news.release/atus.nr0.htm; American Time Use Survey Summary 2012, Bureau of Labor Statistics, US Department of Labor

hours every day. I have increased my reading speed by fifty percent by practicing only ten minutes a day. Thanks to my improved skill, I still can read two hours, and I can absorb monthly, twenty two and a half hours of additional materials. Or I can read the same amount of materials and use all those hours in any way I want. If I would use them for additional work with my present wages, I could earn monthly, an additional two hundred and ten dollars.

On your timer, you have the number of seconds it took you to read the above 344 words. Convert the minutes into seconds, if necessary, and count the words per minute. Use the formula:

344/ number of seconds * 60

Now, you know your reading speed and can make a rational decision about improving it by implementing my advice.

Use my Speed Reading Profits Calculator to check your potential gains. Just provide your reading tempo (words per minute) and how much time you spend reading every day in minutes. If you also add your hourly wage, you will see a monetary equivalent of the time saved. Go and see for yourself: http://www.onedollartips.com/tools/srpcalc

Using my very conservative assumptions, here are some profitability boundaries regarding a 10-minute daily speed reading practice:

A reading tempo (words per minute)	Estimated improvement achieved by 10-minute practice	Daily time spend on reading (minutes)
Less than 250	50%	31
From 250 to 300	40%	37
From 300 to 350	30%	45
From 350 to 400	20%	65
More than 400	10%	120

If you read less than 30 minutes a day, it is pointless to invest 10 minutes and increase your reading speed by 50%. You'll read faster, but you'll also reduce your reading time because of practice. However, you may make bigger progress than me: 60% or 160% and still get a positive net result. It's your call.

On the other hand, the more you read, the more profitable an increase of your reading skill will be. If I read four hours a day, I would save one working week per month.

Conclusion

Check out your reading speed. Estimate how much time you spend reading on average. Find out if a 10-minute practice is viable for you.

10 Minutes

I KNOW that daily, sustained action brings results.

I know it because I do practice this rule in many areas of my life. I focus daily on specific actions, committing 10 minutes to them. I do track my results. And I do see them improving. I've gotten results in such different areas as weight loss, finances, learning skills, and relationships. I strongly believe that it is a universal law applicable to absolutely ALL areas of life.

If you do something daily and you are not getting the desired results, it simply means you are putting at least as much daily and sustained effort against those results.

The more action, the better results - take a look at a chart below.

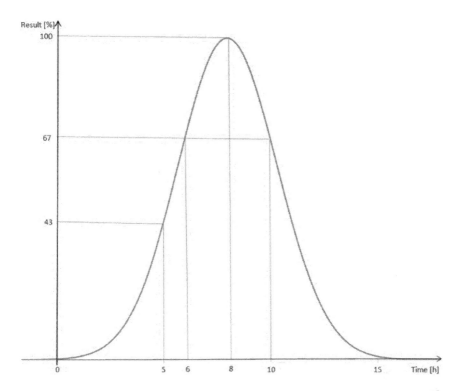

The shape of the curve is called normal distribution in probability research. It is in statistics something like a number π in math. As π can be found in many equations describing the texture of the universe, normal distribution can be used to describe a multitude of quantities in physics and measurements in biology, including IQ, height, weight and many more. According to the central limit theorem, the mean of a large number of random variables tends to normal distribution. And, in our big and complicated world, a lot of effects are presented by a large number of random data. I did study the statistics (years ago) and still don't understand most of this stuff, and it's out of the scope of this book, anyway. If you are curious, it is

12

explained in a forthright way here:
http://askville.amazon.com/Central-Limit-THeorem-apply-statistics-life/AnswerViewer.do?requestId=7620607

I believe the normal distribution can also be applied to describe a relation between a human effort represented by time and achieved results. We have to sleep, so we have about sixteen hours at our disposal, and we can get maximum result investing half of them in one activity. If we give less time, we don't achieve maximum result, and if we dedicate too much time, we are burning out. In the case of speed reading practice, it is quite possible that optimum time is much shorter than eight hours - eyes really hurt after a period of intense training.

But you are not going to devote eight hours a day of your precious life to get a maximum result, which in this case would be ... a world speed reading championship, I suppose. You just need to improve your reading skills. Check out the left part of the chart.

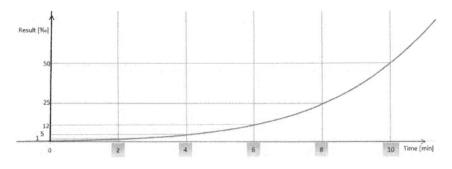

Even the smallest amount of invested time brings results. I use consciously about two minutes of my day on savings, and I do a few monthly activities - a budget summary, paying bills, dividing my resources between different assets, and so on - it takes me about two hours, so overall, it's six minutes a day, and it brings me the results. I've saved almost five times more than a year ago.

So, why is it the Ten-Minute Philosophy? I find that 10 minutes is a nice, easy number. It can even be two minutes, and you will still see results, if it is two minutes of sustained, daily action. With two minutes of course, the results will be smaller; the compounded effect will take about 50 times longer to materialize than with 10 minutes of daily work.

Every - even the tiniest - sustained action brings result.

This truth is the core of my philosophy – this approach will always triumph over the two major obstacles of any lasting change: fear of failure and giving up. Fear of failure stops you before you begin; giving up stops you some time later, but usually happens before the compounding results have become visible.

Every action brings results in the end. As long as you apply sustained energy to something, you can't fail. You have nothing to fear. You **can** start working toward your goals without the burden of hesitations and doubts.

If you believe, if you **know** that every sustained action brings results, giving up is out of the question and any incentives for resignation disappear.

"Alright," you say. "I get the theories, but how are they applicable to my life?" I concur, theorizing doesn't drive results. What led me to embrace this philosophy wasn't stories or the preaching of others. It was my own experience.

In order to feel at a gut level that it is indeed a universal law, applicable also to you, please give a thought to any successful area of your life. It can be anything - your marriage, a specific skill, a career, the fact that you have never had a car accident, good grades at school, patience, your great relationship with your parents. The best thing for this little exercise will be something you take for granted, but other people are praising you for. So, pick one and think: what makes you successful in this area? What's the difference between you and the people who praise you, who aren't successful? What do you do that they don't?

I bet you will find some sustained action underlying your success.

I took for granted the love in my family. I hadn't noticed that it was anything special until my newfound online friends drew my attention to it through their comments on my personal blog. I gave it some thought and saw the sustained action. I tell my wife and kids I love them every day.

And this is just one instance of this law. I have found many other examples behind my big and small successes - my high-school diploma, the scholarship I received for my 4th year of university studies, my personal fitness progress.

It is true. You will find such examples in your life, too.

Look at the time/results chart once again. You probably noticed how the results grow exponentially after some point. As I said earlier - the more time you invest, the better results you get. I'm assuming that speed reading is not your first priority, so you don't want to invest much time. I understand you have your family to take care of, bills to pay, work to do, people to help, projects to attend to, relationships to keep or improve. A speed reading practice comes after all of those activities in your life, so it's natural you read at average speed. You have more pressing matters to take care of. You have only twenty four hours, and it's hard to find time for anything else. Thus, 10 minutes.

Speed Reading Obstacles

Unfortunately, the vast amount of knowledge we have gathered as humans seems to guarantee that we have at least two opinions about every single thing. Just look at the various diets and fitness strategies: eat that - no, eat this; eat in the morning - no, eat in the afternoon; eat fruits on an empty stomach - no, use them as snacks; run or walk steadily for half an hour every day - no, use five minute HIIT training every second day. It seems we can't agree on anything. It's the same with speed reading.

One study shows that sub-vocalization is an unavoidable part of reading process and doesn't affect reading speed; another shows that it's necessary to reduce it to the point of elimination to improve reading speed. One shows that listening to music while reading can improve your speed; another that it slows you down.

Frankly, I don't care what the latest research "proved" this time. I'm a practitioner. So, I'm teaching what worked in my case and in the case of other people with whom I have contact. I have no interest in the opinions of eggheads as long as they are contradictory to each other, and especially when they are contradictory with my experiences.

Thus, I do not quote authorities and research studies in this book. I just show you what my beliefs are, what techniques I use ... and what results I get.

Ok, so now let's go for the reasons of less than optimal reading speed.

Sub-vocalization.

Sub-vocalization, or silent speech, is defined as the internal speech made when reading a word, thus allowing the reader to imagine the sound of the word as it is read. This is a natural process when reading - but **only** because we all were taught to read by vocalization first.

Sub-vocalization is popularly associated with moving one's lips; the actual term refers primarily to the movement of muscles associated with speaking, not the literal moving of lips. Most sub-vocalization is done just inside our heads and is undetectable even by the person doing the sub-vocalizing.

The definition of sub-vocalization that I found states also that it "helps to reduce cognitive load, and it helps the mind to access meanings to enable it to comprehend and remember what is read." And I say, "That's B.S."

I achieved the biggest improvement in reading speed by applying the sub-vocalization reducing exercises. We don't read through our ears; we read through our eyes. "Translating" letters and words to sounds slows us down. When we do that, the talking speed reduces our reading speed. Speed reading is about getting information straight from the sheet of paper (or a screen) through our eyes to our brain. Sense of hearing as a go-between is redundant.

Fixation

Reading is not a process of recognizing a text word by word; it's recognizing the meaning of the words in context.

Try to	Isn't it a	easily	your eyes
read this	mental effort	comprehend	run all over
text normally	making your	those sentences	the text
as usual,	head spin?	in that way.	and your mind
from left	It's very	You are	is trying to
to right.	difficult to	confused,	figure the meaning out.

Most of us don't realize that the eye sees the picture **only** when it is motionless. While reading, if the eye "jumps" from one part of text to another, it's called an eye fixation. The more fixations you do, the slower you read. There are a few elements which determine your number of fixations.

Vision span

Your eye's efficiency is very important in the reading process. If your vision span is wider, you can read more words per fixation. That means fewer fixations per text line and higher speed of reading. And opposite dependency is also true - since each fixation equals less words read, then the more fixations per line equals slower reading progress. Vision span is a physical attribute, and it can be trained.

Vocabulary

To see how vocabulary determines eye fixations, try to read the verses below carefully, to get their meaning:

Sownynge in moral vertu was his speche,
And gladly wolde he lerne, and gladly teche.

These lines come from "The Cantebury Tales", written in Middle English in the 14th century by Geoffrey Chaucer.

You had problems with comprehending this text because some of the words are not in your vocabulary. When you are not familiar with a text, you read and you don't know the words used, your eyes stop frequently to recognize the unfamiliar meaning and the number of fixations increases.

When you don't need to dwell on specific words, you read more words in one fixation, which allows you to read faster.

Compare your speed of understanding Middle English verses with the speed of reading below:

Filled with moral virtue was his speech,
And gladly would he learn, and gladly teach.

It was much easier and faster this time, wasn't it?

Topic familiarity

Your background, your education, your interests, your general knowledge - all these factors influence your reading speed, because they determine your vocabulary and your reading confidence. When the topic is familiar to you, is in your area of expertise or field of interest, you are at home with the author's terminology. The overall meaning is obvious to you, so again, you don't dwell on individual words, and you need fewer fixations to read a single line. Thus, you read faster.

It explains the paradox of correlation between reading speed and comprehension. The lesser understanding of text leads to the slower reading. On the other hand, the faster you read, the more you can read and you can get familiar with more subjects.

Regression

It simply means back-tracking, re-reading text that you've already read. It's like taking two steps forward and one step back with your eyes. The reasons for regression can differ from one case to another: lack of concentration, really difficult text to comprehend, an excessive sub-vocalization – which disrupts the process of reading – or just bad reading habits.

Other

Different "schools" of speed reading numerate many different additional reasons: lack of concentration, lighting, lack of selection and anticipation skills, and lack of reading tactics. All of these are obvious generalizations or some extensions of sub-vocalization, fixation or regression.

For example, a lack of concentration. Well, it's normal that you get worse results if you are not concentrating, no matter if you read or make burgers at McDonald's. Lighting is important – you cannot read in the dark, can you? Selection and anticipation skills are related to topic familiarity and vocabulary. You cannot select main points from a text when you don't know what it is talking about; you cannot anticipate the meaning of words when your vocabulary is poor. Undeveloped selection and anticipation skills also drive you into regression – if you don't fully comprehend what you read, you try to get the meaning by re-reading a fragment of the text.

Techniques

The way we learn to read is the cause of every problem we have with speed reading. It is like our training had been aborted in the middle. We all learn at school to read by going through various stages: first recognizing the letters, then joining them into groups and spelling them out, then reading out loud to get a smoothness in reading skill, and finally, we learn to read internally, using our mind's voice. And our teachers are perfectly comfortable with that: "Can Johnny read? Yes, great! Next one!" And we are left at this socially acceptable level of reading skill.

I say, if some simple techniques were to be introduced into primary school's syllabus, all children would have improved reading speed.

I will numerate a few techniques to fight off every speed reading obstacle and explain which I've chosen them for my practice and why.

Sub-vocalization

To reduce sub-vocalization, you need to stop using your sense of hearing to read. All of the exercises below help you to replace the old, slow "see–say–hear–think" way of reading with the faster "see–think" habit of **thinking word meanings**.

Bite your tongue

It is a first, basic technique. It is possible to apply only if you read really slowly, and you are able to observe that you are trying to articulate words while reading - you murmur or move your tongue, consciously or subconsciously.

My son, who used to read very slowly, used this technique successfully.

Occupy your internal voice with another task

- count aloud as you read "1, 2, 3, 4, 5, 6" and so on
-hum
-sing something simple like "la-la-la-la"
-recite simple and very deeply memorized text
And my favorite: **beat a rhythm as you read**.
I have no intention of acting like a blusterous lunatic while reading. I read mostly at work or in a public transport. There are people around me most of the time. But beating a rhythm is a whole different story. It is unobtrusive, so I read and pat my thigh rhythmically.

What is more, the workbook's author claims this method is the most difficult and most effective for reducing sub-vocalization. Nothing but advantages - so I adopted it.

I just recall some melody and use its rhythm. I found also that actually hearing a rhythm is not necessary. I travel in noisy trains and buses a lot. Sometimes, so noisy that I can't hear my own patting. But the act of patting makes me concentrate on a rhythm and hear the "sound" of the rhythm in my head.

It's important to use your whole forearm, not just a wrist. Beating transfers a part of your attention from the hearing sense to your body motion.

Don't get frustrated if the art of reading and occupying your internal voice simultaneously eludes you. It's normal. You will lose a rhythm focusing too much on comprehending a text. You will beat a rhythm perfectly, but you will lose an ability to focus on reading. You will have no idea what you have just read after the exercise. The same is true with other tactics - recitation, singing, humming, and counting aloud.

Sub-vocalization: conclusion

Using one of the above techniques is obligatory if you want to improve your reading speed. Sub-vocalization is the number one enemy of speed reading. "See–say–hear–think" is a detour we have been taught as children, and it will not serve you right in adulthood. Breaking this habitual detour is a pesky experience, but the results are well worth it.

Fixation

There are lots of causes of a greater number of fixations, so there is no single simple remedy to fix it.

Whatever the people behind the speed reading industry – the people who are selling the books, programs, and courses say – nobody can substitute for you. You are the one who needs to work on your vocabulary or topic familiarity. Techniques can help you only in the "technical" aspect. You can expand your vision span with exercises, but it won't do you much good, if you don't understand every third word in some professional periodical.

Eye span pyramid

There are different kinds of pyramids - with single words, sentences, and numbers. You are supposed to read them from the apex to the bottom, keeping your view in the middle of the pyramid. The vertical moves of eyeballs are not allowed.

This

exercise

will help you

to expand your vision

span by working on your

peripheral vision. You can read

more words at a time when your vision span is wider

When the text is too wide for you to read it with one fixation, then stop, close your eyes for a few seconds, open them again focusing your view in the middle of the pyramid, and try to see as many words as possible on the both sides of the line.

Shultz tables

This is a tool to train your vision span. A table consists of 25 fields filled with symbols. They are usually numbers, but they also can be letters or any kind of symbols that can be arranged in a specific order. Doing exercises with Shultz tables develops your three-dimensional, multi-channeled attention. The symbols in the table will subconsciously be perceived as one picture.

6	13	19	17	2
11	22	8	25	23
18	16	1	20	12
14	10	24	15	5
4	7	21	9	3

Your purpose is to concentrate your view on the center field, whilst being able to see the central number and all the numbers in the corners of a table. Then, you find the numbers in ascending or descending order as fast as you can, keeping your view focused on the central square of the table.

At the beginning, you can start with smaller tables - 3x3 or 4x4 fields. You should be able to point out all numbers in less than one minute. Try to find the numbers faster with each successive exercise.

I like Shultz tables the most of all the exercises expanding the field of vision. They are relatively easy to create, and numbers in each of them are arranged in a random manner. It is not so easy to randomly create pyramids or columns of words or numbers. I found some PDF documents, printed them and used them for the practice sessions. After several iterations, I had all the text and numbers memorized and couldn't use them effectively.

Fixation training

The next stage of expanding your vision span is to create a fixation habit. To have a wide vision span is fine and good, but we were taught to read a text word by word, so we need to develop new reading habits - to jump just a few times over a text line with our eyesight. I've just started this kind of training - this is as far as my personal program has gotten so far.

You should develop the habit of moving your eyesight just a couple times per line. I used pre-prepared texts and, more or less, I memorized them. To work on a new text with every practice session, you need a template with dots marking the stopping points for your eye. It's a little fuss to copy a new text to a template file and print it every time, but it's much better than working on a text you've already read several times.

This kind of reading also helps tremendously with fighting off a regression. You consciously force yourself to read chunks of text jumping from one to another, and there is no going back in this method.

You train this way of reading as long as it's necessary to develop a new subconscious habit.

Fixation: conclusion

No "technical" exercises will help you to enrich your vocabulary or general knowledge. You must work on them on your own. If you worked on some text previously a couple of times, the training of your eyes transforms into the training of your memory. You need a source of fresh reading materials for your practice sessions.

Regression

Regression can slow you down significantly. If you read very fast, but you need to go back and re-read the text you've just gone through, then in consequence, you read at a mediocre pace.

The picture below illustrates how your eyes are working when a regression takes place:

What you need instead, is steady movement in one direction. Always forward.

Selection

Conscious control over your attention is an important part of speed reading. Selection, paying your attention to a specific purpose, is a skill that can help you to decide if scanned text is useful for you and worth reading or not. It is especially important in the Internet era.

Selection exercises are really simple, and I love them because you can work on any text. Well, almost any – the text you practice on must be new to you.

Exercises:

- within five seconds, find a repeated word in a text. Read the text to the end, counting the occurrences of this word

- find all the articles in a text

- find all the numbers in a text

- find all the connectives in a text

- find all the verbs in a text

And you can establish your own criteria of selection. The only limit is your creativity. It all comes down to finding something in a text. You can also add a time factor to the exercises; for example, you have only 20 seconds to find all the articles on a page.

Pointer

I left the best for last. Using a pointer to read has a multitude of advantages. It helps to eliminate regression, reduce sub-vocalization, and to master your eye fixation. It is THE technique of speed reading.

Using a pointer is the most powerful and easiest way to eliminate a regression. Use the tip of your finger or a pen. Point it below the line of text and move it as you read in a sweeping motion, just like kids who learn to read. Oh, a little faster than them. You don't have to point the whole length of a line, your peripheral vision will take care of the beginnings and ends of the lines.

Reading above the speed of your usual comprehension rate with a pointer reduces sub-vocalization. Your internal voice just cannot cope with your pointer.

Pursuing the pointer with your eyesight, especially faster than you are used to reading, trains your eyes to catch chunks of sentences, not individual words.

This one simple tool may have an enormous influence on your reading skill progress.

If you read mostly on a computer screen - like me - don't worry. Use the pointer for your practice sessions and whenever you lay hands on a paper copy. The progress might not be as rapid as you wish, but there will be some progress, nonetheless. Your exercises with physical books will improve your screen reading, too.

You can also use a pointer to read from eReader devices, unless they have touch panels. But there is a work-around for such devices, too – just hover the pointer a quarter of an inch over the device. By the way, that's the way I prefer to use a pointer. I find the swish of the finger on a paper sheet a bit distracting.

My workbook encouraged me to start by sweeping the pointer every second line, and try to read two lines at a time, then to read three, four, and more, and then go to even more advanced techniques.

Regression: conclusion

There are other, more advanced techniques for eliminating regression, but I haven't used them yet. And I'm already 10 months into my 10-minute speed reading program. They are not needed at the beginning; there is a lot of time for you to look for them later.

You can train selection on any unknown text.

Using the pointer is the simplest and most powerful speed reading technique (if you can even call it technique). It's just something we don't usually do during "ordinary" reading, but we should.

Don't worry if you read mostly from a computer screen; use the pointer for your practice sessions only, and it will impact your screen reading, too.

Super speed exercises

Those exercises are not humanly possible to execute, especially the first one, when your task is to read a little faster than your record. Even if you read 4,700 words per minute (about world record), you should exercise reading faster than that. The goal of those exercises is to strain your "reading muscle" so it can grow.

1. The whole single iteration of this exercise takes about 8-10 minutes.

a) for one minute, read with a speed greater than 100 words per minute than your actual record

b) for one minute, read with a speed greater than 100 words per minute than in point a)

c) for one minute, read with a speed greater than 100 words per minute than in point b)

d) for one minute, read with a speed greater than 100 words per minute than in point c)

e) for one minute, read with a speed greater than 100 words per minute than in point d)

f) for one minute, read with comprehension as fast as you can

2. This exercise takes about 20 minutes. I only do it on weekends, when I can organize more time for my practice sessions.

a) for one minute, read using a pointer with a speed 2,000 words per minute. Sweep the pointer every three, four, or more lines. Mark the point where you finished reading.

I used "Iliad" and "Odyssey" for this practice. I figured out that one page contains about 250 words, so I was supposed to read eight pages within a minute.

b) read again the same fragment of text as in point a), but use 4 minutes this time

c) read again the same fragment of text within 3 minutes

d) read again the same fragment of text within 2 minutes

e) read for 5 minutes in a way described in point a) from the text you marked onward (it was 40 more pages in my case)

f) for one minute read with comprehension as fast as you can

3. This exercise takes about 5-6 minutes.

a) start from beginning of the chapter: scan the text using the pointer; you have 4 seconds to scan each page

b) read the text scanned in point a) with the speed of 2000 words per minute

c) for one minute, read with comprehension as fast as you can

4. The whole single iteration of this exercise takes less than 3 minutes.

a) for one minute, read as fast as you can; don't care about comprehending what you read

b) for one minute, read with comprehension as fast as you can

Program

The first thing to do is to gauge your reading speed. You probably already know this after reading chapter 1.

The results you get can vary from one test to another. They are dependent not only on your level of reading skill, but also on external conditions: lighting, noise level and so on. Even your mood and the kind of text on which you are taking a test can influence the results. My reading speed varies from 360 to 510 words per minute – the difference is huge, isn't it?

I recommend that you gauge your reading speed at least once a week, ideally in the same circumstances. For example, in the morning next to the window, with a lot of sunlight. Or, you can measure it every day and take the average. I don't recommend this approach, because gauging takes time, too, and we are talking about a 10-minute program here.

If you are determined to measure your reading speed every day, I recommend using the below, approximated (and fast) method:

- count the number of words on five consecutive full lines of print. (for example, 55 words on five lines)

- divide this by 5 to get an average number of words per line. (for example, 11 words per line)

- set the timer for a minute

- read for one minute and count the number of lines (for example, 35 lines read)

- multiple the number of lines you have read by the average words per line (for example, 35*11=385 words per minute)

For more gauging methods, visit my blog.

Use easy and interesting lectures for your practices. I practice on books "I've always wanted to read, but have never had time to do it."

"Warm up" your eyes. It is supposed to sharpen your vision and activate your peripheral sight. Just trace the geometric figure or infinity symbol with your eyes alone and then switch, moving your eyes in the other direction. Experts advise to do it for one minute; I do it for 10 to 20 seconds before each practice session.

I remind you that I've tailored an intensive speed reading self-course to 10 minute practices. You can do the same with my program. For example, you can use 30 minutes for daily practices and shrink every program's stage to one month.

Stage 1. Months one to three

1. Reducing the sub-vocalization.

Check out the techniques I described in chapter 4. Try various methods, and choose the one best suited for you.

2. Super speed exercise number 1.

I recommend to practice it 1-2 times a week. Remember, use the pointer.

Stage 2. Months four to six

1. Continue the exercises for reducing the sub-vocalization.

- if you have chosen some other method, try the rhythm beating exercise once a week; it is supposed to be the most effective way to fight off sub-vocalization.

- focus on the comprehension

2. Selection exercises.

3. Super speed exercise number 2.

Stage 3. Months seven to nine.

1. Eye span training.

- Shultz tables

- eye span pyramids

2. Super speed exercise number 3.

Stage 4. Months ten to twelve.

1. Continue the eye span widening exercises.

2. Fixation training.

3. Super speed exercise number 4.

A call to action

And that's as far as my training got. Nothing fancy, is it?

You may find other good, solid advice on how to arrange your speed reading practice sessions:

- secure the proper environment: lighting, peace and quiet for your sessions
- concentrate
- sit upright
- be alone
- use the professional tools and programs
- take care of your mental attitude: realize the goal of every session and overall program, set your mind to do the exercises to the best of your abilities
- set your own goals and deadlines

All of this is fine, all is good, but there is one missing ingredient: you. All that advice can discourage you. It looks like a lot of fuss, doesn't it? You must prepare: close yourself in your private office, meditate to clear and focus your mind, and then, practice speed reading, for 19 minutes. Do you feel motivated by such a picture?

The above advice is important but not critical. You can practice in a noisy environment; you can practice with inappropriate lighting; you can practice with diminished focus; or you can be discouraged. How do I know? Well, I've been there, done that.

I'm occupied with so many projects that I have no time to arrange my speed reading practice sessions. I practice on the fly - while commuting, whenever I read something which demands less than 100% of my attention (I developed a beating habit). I can practice in a "sterile atmosphere" only on weekends, when I wake up before other family members, and I do my super speed exercises in peace and quiet.

You will fail **only** if you don't practice. The whole idea of this book is to show you that speed reading is not rocket science. In fact, it's quite mundane. And it's easy. Do you know Jim Rohn's definition of "easy?" It's something you can do.

And in fact, you can do it. It's just like your reading education had been aborted halfway in primary school. My 10-year-old son improved his reading speed by more than double what it had been – are your skills worse than a child's? Ten minutes a day is enough to observe some progress within a few weeks. It's worth it. You can read more. You can spend less time on reading. You can use the saved time to play with your children, spend it with your spouse, or do whatever else you want.

So start. Persevere. Keep practicing. It will feel awkward, especially at the beginning. You won't grasp what you read on your early sessions, or on super speed exercises. Don't worry. Keep pushing. Remember, daily sustained action brings results. It's a law of nature.

Free Resources

There are a lot of books, courses, and computer programs on the Internet regarding speed reading. Some of them advertise their services giving some free resources. And you English speakers are blessed with useful tools freely available on the Net.

While writing this booklet, I've done some research and found several amazing tools for English readers. I will also give you some links to my own resources. I can't guarantee that the tools that are not mine will be available and free forever - those are just some resources I stumbled upon during my research.

Those are not affiliate links, I don't try to sell you anything. I didn't test any paid services on the sites I linked to. I just tested some free tools and found them helpful. Below, I'll list them and comment on how you can use them.

http://www.eyercize.com/practice/bm_read - very useful tool for fixation training. I love its flexibility - you can set the reading speed, the number of fixations, number of words per fixation and a few more things. The best feature is that you can train each time on a different text. You just press the "New" button and paste your text. The only critical remark I have is that the window with the text is not very wide, and the text can be broken in a weird way.

You can also use it for super speed exercises 1 and 2. Setting the reading speed makes it soooo easy.

http://spreeder.com/ - it has similar features as the previous tool - you can paste your own text and set a reading speed - but it projects just a few words at a time, you can't see more than a single line of text at once.

http://www.readability.com - great tool to improve your comfort with online reading. It converts any web page into a plain, black and white nicely formatted presentation of the text. It removes all distractions - ads, links, unnecessary images, and videos.

It doesn't work perfectly - on one portal it generated the same article three times for me. You can use it as a stand-alone application or as an add-on to the Firefox browser.

http://fasterreader.eu/pages/en/index-en.html - They have a whole bunch of tools there, most of them are Java-based which causes some trouble in Firefox browser.

- fine tool for selection training

- tool for warming up your eyes - use it before practice if you practice in front of a computer.

- vision span training on Shultz's tables - fine tool with the element of a game; unfortunately, clicking on numbers perturbs your concentration on the center of the table.

- figures for warm up exercises - on my site; you can print it and use for offline practices; just follow the dots with your eyesight very fast in one direction, then again in another direction.

- Shultz's tables generator - on my site; it generates random tables for offline practice. I use them for my own practices. It's not very user friendly, but it does its job. I prefer 5x5 dimensions of the tables. To generate new set of tables, just press the "back" button in the browser and press the "generate" button once again. Try different browsers and different printer settings to get an ideal size on the paper sheet.

The Stories

I've promised you stories, so here they are. Most of mine you know from the first chapter, although I've filled in some blanks. I include my son's story, also. Nathaniel is 10 years old and had significant problems with reading. He more than doubled his reading speed within eight months.

Nathaniel's Story

At the first parent teacher meeting of the school year of 2012-2013, (18th of October 2012) I discovered that my son was neglecting his school work. Let's keep quiet about the home scene which took place after the meeting. It was too ugly to be printed ;)

Anyway, I decided to pay more attention to his learning. He hated to read. In fact, he hated it so much that we used to give him reading assignments as a punishment.

The day after the parent-teacher meeting, I gauged his reading speed. The result were very poor, even for ten years old - just 71 words per minute. He had been sub-vocalizing quite audibly, murmuring under his nose. So, we started a reading practice program. He first had to read five, then ten pages a day. I advised him to bite his tongue while reading.

We did a next test of his reading speed on the last day of October. He improved to 100 words per minute within twelve days. A 42% increase; not too bad.

At the end of November, he read 130 words per minute. I set him the goal for the end of January: 150 words per minute. But he got stuck. He was still below this boundary at the end of March.

I insisted on a technique he doesn't like - beating rhythmically while reading, as I got great results doing it rigorously. He has been doing it very unwillingly.

In the middle of April, we were preparing for another speed reading test, when I proposed:

"Use your finger as a pointer" - this is another basic technique, but I just had never mentioned it to him before. I had been focusing on eliminating his excessive sub-vocalization, neglecting other enemies of speed reading.

"OK" - he agreed hesitantly. He had never done it before.

And BAM! His result was 170 words per minute!

It was a great result.

So, we made an agreement that, from then on, I would not supervise his reading. He could read as much (or not as much) as he wanted. I scheduled the next test at the end of May, and he happily neglected his speed reading training. He trained maybe 10 times within the whole month. Every sustained action brings results, but his action was not consistent. His reading speed dived below 170 words per minute again.

The next test, on the 10th of May, didn't show any improvement, so I again made him read every day. At the end of May, he read 192 words per minute – his best results so far.

He has read all seven parts of "The Chronicles of Narnia" and four other books during the training process. That is more books than 70% of Americans, ages 16 and up, have read in 2012[2]

My story

When I started my self-development program, I'd stumbled upon a workbook about speed reading. The author outlined a program there for a massive improvement in the speed of reading within three months, but you were supposed to practice 1-2 hours per day, every day.

Two hours per day! That's a lot of commitment. About 25% of my available time. And I need that time to commute, to spend with family, to pray, and to learn other skills. Out of the question.

But I had fresh in my mind all the examples of consistent fruitful efforts from my past, so I gave my 10 minutes philosophy a chance. "I'll only practice fast reading for 10 minutes a day," I decided. Why not? It was just 10 minutes. So, I took that program and modified it by extending each week into 12 weeks.

---

http://libraries.pewinternet.org/2012/12/27/e-book-reading-jumps-print-book-reading-declines/

The program from the workbook I found starts with exercises eliminating sub-vocalization. I read a lot, so I have plenty of opportunities to practice, but beating rhythmically while reading made me dizzy. Either I didn't understand what I was reading, or I couldn't keep the rhythm. One way or another, the practice was no fun. Nevertheless, I stuck with this exercise for a few weeks.

The last time I had checked my reading speed was during my university study. I read about 240 words per minute. Since that time, my skills had no chance to improve, as I was reading less rather than more and neglected any training in that area.

I checked my results after a month from starting my 10-minute practice, and I was blown away! It was 360 words per minute, a 50% progress! One month, 30 short sessions of practice, and I was able to read 50% more books in the same time. Later on, it appeared this result was just coincidence. Reading speed varies from one test to another; it is dependent on the text I'm testing on, my mood, and external circumstances. But still, after six weeks of practice, I read about 340 words per minute, and the progress was impressive.

You can't even imagine what it meant to me. I'm a reader. I had read thousands of books with my meager 240-words-per-minute speed. Suddenly, I felt like a kid in a candy store when a 50% bargain sale was announced. To get the picture of my state at that moment, try to recall Gollum from the Lord of the Rings, drooling and lisping, "my pressssscious."

From that moment on, I had no hesitation at all. I've been going through the next stages of the program, without flinching. I used the practice sessions to read some classic books I had never had time for: Homer's *Iliad* and *Odyssey*, Clausewitz's *On War*, Napoleon Hill's *Think and Grow Rich*, and several others. I am reading Marcus Aurelius' *Meditations* now.

When it came to the selection skill practices, I used those sessions to read Early to Rise newsletters, which had piled up in my mailbox. I skipped the text looking for the articles or conjunctions, and I was able to get the meaning, by the way.

My results have regularly been above 360 words per minute for several months. The best results I've gotten was 511 words per minute, and I'm reaching over 400 words quite often.

Conclusion

When I read the stories of people who improved their reading skills by 100% within a few weeks, I feel a little dumb. My progress is meager and slow compared to them. But I really practice just 10 minutes a day. I do 90% of my reading on a computer screen; the only pointer I can use, in this case, is a mouse cursor, and it is not the most comfortable tool for this job.

I'm living proof that a 10-minute practice can be fruitful. I can read more than 50% of what I read a year ago within the same time. I can read 90 minutes a day (including the speed reading practices) and still read the same amount of text that used to take me two hours to read a year ago.

You can do it, too. Do yourself a favor. Save your reading time for more interesting activities. Read much more in the same amount of time, and improve your skills and knowledge. And you can get much better and more rapid results than me. Practice 20 minutes a day, instead of 10. Practice in optimal conditions, not on noisy, crowded buses. Just be more serious in your training than I was, and you are bound to progress faster.

Value your time. Your time is your life. Start today, grab a book and use your finger as a pointer, or read and simultaneously pat your thigh rhythmically. Just for ten minutes. Discover that there is no magic in speed reading and keep practicing.

A Favor Please

I used to actively discourage my readers from giving me a review immediately after they read my book. I asked you for a review only once you began seeing results. This approach was against common sense and standard practice. Reviews are crucial for a book's visibility on Amazon. And my approach severely hindered me from getting my message out to people just like you, who stand to benefit from it.

I was convinced about that when "Master Your Time in 10 Minutes a Day" became a best-seller. Essentially, I've gotten a number of reviews in a short amount of time, but most of those reviews were the 'plastic' ones we all dislike on Amazon: "Great book! Great content! Great reading! Great entertainment!" Such reviews simply don't carry much weight; anybody could leave a review like that without even reading the book.

In the end, it didn't matter, and my book skyrocketed up the best-seller ranks, anyway. More people than ever have had the chance to get my book in their hands. I'm grateful for this, because more people have received the means to take control over their time and their destiny.

I want to ask a favor of you. If you have found value in this book, please take a moment and share your opinion with the world. Just let me know what you learned and how it affected you in a positive way. Your reviews help me to positively change the lives of others. Thank you!

Contact Me

I'd love to know your reading skills progress and see that my work has helped you some way, so please send me a simple email saying, "I used to read xxx words per minute, and now I read yyy wpm," to speedreading@onedollartips.com. That's all I need, although any other feedback is always welcomed as well. You can also follow me at www.expandbeyondyourself.com

About the Author

I'm Michal Stawicki and I live in Poland, Europe. I've been married for over 14 years and am the father of two boys and one girl. I work full time in the IT industry, and recently, I've become an author. My passions are transparency, integrity and progress.

In August 2012, I read a book called "The Slight Edge" by Jeff Olson. It took me a whole month to start implementing ideas from this book. That led me to reading numerous other books on personal development, some effective, some not so much. I took a look at myself and decided this was one person who could surely use some development.

In November of 2012, I created my personal mission statement; I consider it the real starting point of my progress. Over several months time, I applied several self-help concepts and started building inspiring results: I lost some weight, greatly increased my savings, built new skills and got rid of bad habits while developing better ones.

I'm very pragmatic, a "down to earth" person. I favor utilitarian, bottom-line results over pure artistry. Despite the ridiculous language, however, I found there is value in the "hokey-pokey visualization" stuff and I now see it as my mission to share what I have learned.

My books are not abstract. I avoid going mystical as much as possible. I don't believe that pure theory is what we need in order to change our lives; the Internet age has proven this quite clearly. What you will find in my books are:

- detailed techniques and methods describing how you can improve your skills and drive results in specific areas of your life

- real life examples

- personal stories

So, whether you are completely new to personal development or have been crazy about the Law of Attraction for years, if you are looking for concrete strategies, you will find them in my books. My writing shows that I am a relatable, ordinary guy and not some ivory tower guru.